Bull Sharks

by Grace Hansen

abdopublishing.com

Published by Abdo Kids, a division of ABDO, PO Box 398166, Minneapolis, Minnesota 55439.

Copyright © 2016 by Abdo Consulting Group, Inc. International copyrights reserved in all countries. No part of this book may be reproduced in any form without written permission from the publisher.

Printed in the United States of America, North Mankato, Minnesota.

102015

012016

 THIS BOOK CONTAINS
RECYCLED MATERIALS

Photo Credits: iStock, Minden Pictures, Science Source, Seapics.com, Shutterstock, Thinkstock

Production Contributors: Teddy Borth, Jennie Forsberg, Grace Hansen

Design Contributors: Laura Mitchell, Dorothy Toth

Library of Congress Control Number: 2015941987

Cataloging-in-Publication Data

Hansen, Grace.

 Bull sharks / Grace Hansen.

   p. cm. -- (Sharks)

ISBN 978-1-68080-152-1 (lib. bdg.)

Includes index.

1. Bull shark--Juvenile literature.   I. Title.

597.34--dc23

2015941987

Table of Contents

Bull Sharks

Bull sharks live in oceans.

They prefer **shallow**,

warm water. They are

often found in **fresh water**.

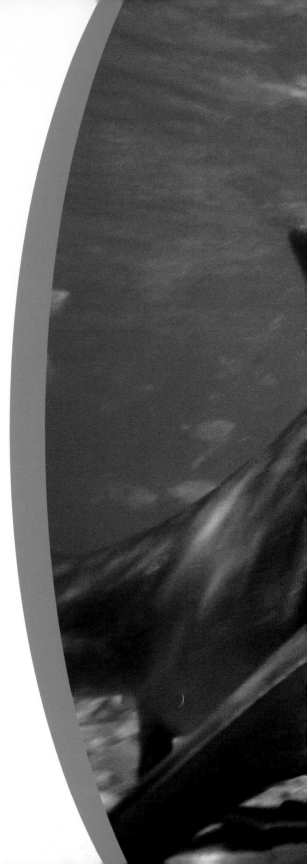

4

Bull sharks have short, round noses. They have small eyes.

Bull sharks have thick
bodies. They can grow
to be 11 feet (3.4 m) long.

Bull sharks are mostly gray.

They have white bellies.

Some have black-tipped fins.

11

Bull sharks move slowly along the ocean floor. But they can be quick. This makes them good hunters.

Food & Hunting

Bull sharks hunt during the day and night. They usually hunt alone. They sometimes hunt in groups.

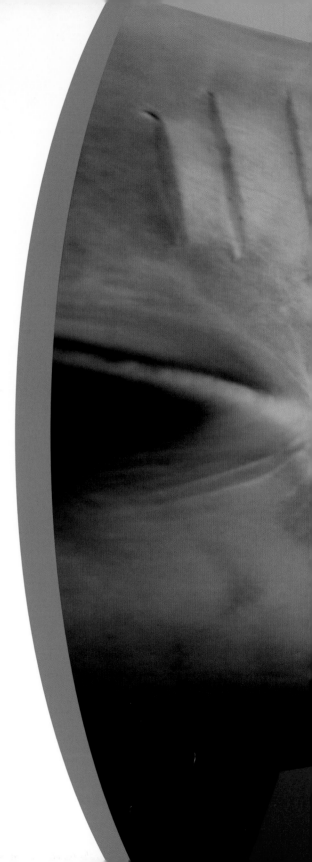

Bull sharks mostly eat

fish and small sharks.

They also eat crabs,

shrimp, and other animals.

Baby Bull Sharks

Baby sharks are called pups. Bull sharks give birth to around 10 pups.

Pups are usually born near **coasts**. **Shallow** water keeps them safe from big **predators**. Pups move to deeper water once they have grown.

21

More Facts

- There are 43 types of sharks that can live in both **fresh water** and salt water. Bull sharks are one of them.

- Females are typically larger and live longer than males.

- Males live around 13 years. Females can live to about 17 years old.

Glossary

coast – the edge of land along the sea.

fresh water – water found in lakes, rivers, and ponds that does not have salt.

predator – an animal that hunts and eats other animals.

shallow – not deep.

Index

abdokids.com

Use this code to log on to abdokids.com and access crafts, games, videos, and more!

Abdo Kids Code:
SBK1521